T.A. for TOTS

for

(and other prinzes)

Transactional Analysis for Everybody Series

T.A. for TOTS
(and other prinzes)

by

Alvyn M. Freed, Ph.D.

JALMAR PRESS INC. Sacramento

1st Printing, 1973: 10,000 books
2nd Printing, 1974: 20,000 books
3rd Printing, 1974: 50,000 books
4th Printing, 1974: 25,000 books
5th Printing, 1974: 25,000 books
6th Printing, 1975: 25,000 books
7th Printing, 1975: 35,000 books
8th Printing, 1976: 50,000 books
9th Printing, 1977: 25,000 books
10th Printing, 1978: 25,000 books
11th Printing, 1979: 25,000 books
12th Printing, 1980: 25,000 books

Published by Jalmar Press, Inc.
6501 Elvas Ave., Sacramento, Ca. 95819

Copyright © by Jalmar Press, Inc.
Printed in the United States of America

All Rights Reserved
ISBN 0-915190-12-5

Library of Congress: 76-19650

illustrations
by
JoAnn Dick

lettering
by
Donna Ferreri

DEDICATION

To my mother, Amy E. Freed, who loves all Tots and whose strokes are so very important to me

To Margaret, my wife, without whose love and understanding, I'd be a Froz

To my sons, Mark and Larry, who, to me, will always be Prinzes

I dedicate this book.

Alwyn M. Freed

ACKNOWLEDGEMENTS

As in all situations where the task is completed in a satisfactory manner, more than one person is responsible. TA for TOTS is no exception.

The text is the author's but without JoAnn Dick, it would be a dull and lifeless thing. With her illustrations and layout, it becomes an exciting and delightful experience. Donna Ferreri, our young art student, gave a sense of spontaneity to the text through her printing.

We wish to acknowledge John Lopes, whose skilled criticism guided us through crucial times. We hope his generous sharing of his professional know-how is reflected in the product.

Also, I wish to acknowledge Sue Baker, secretary, typist, proof reader, critic, encourager, who types and types and types until it's all done.

Thanks to all of you.

CONTENTS

INTRODUCTION

"TA for Tots" (and other prinzes) is the second in the series "TA for Everybody". "TA for Tots" is designed to help little boys and girls get acquainted with themselves, to find out that they are not frogs, but princes and princesses. By talking straight to their mothers and fathers and other important people, they will be able to stay princes and princesses and learn how to get rid of froggy feelings. Then they will be able to avoid some of the unhappiness that most grown-ups now experience. The hope is that they will be able to understand mother daddy, brothers and sisters a lot more clearly than they themselves were understood and that, perhaps through such understanding, they will be able to get along better with these important people. They may even avoid the need for psychotherapy, nervous breakdowns and other things bad for children because they will avoid the "poisons" which people use to turn themselves from princes into frogs. They may be able to learn to avoid providing "poison" for their own youngsters when they grow up.

So, "TA for Tots" and its predecessor "TA for Kids" is the first step, it seems to me, in starting the backfire against mental illness and emotional conflict that seem to be sweeping our civilization. Somewhere someone has said that by the time one is sixteen one must be carefully taught how to be crazy enough to fit into our civilization. Let's change this. By eliminating many of the early frog-producing poisons, children can begin to understand their setting and to deal with it more effectively. Then they will be able to avoid the need to be crazy in order to survive. "TA for Tots" is a second step in that direction.

II

"TA for Tots" is couched in very simple terms. The pictures are designed to hook and stroke the kid. There is enough fun in it to interest and hook most grown-ups and I think you big frogs will find some things which will hook your kid. This is our intent. It is not our intent to be terribly serious. Seriousness belongs in the Parent. Truth is in the Adult. If we can stroke the kid, we have a chance to do something for the Adult because the Adult is where we make sense out of chaos.

A recommendation to mothers and fathers is to hold the young one on your lap, turn on the tape, relax and enjoy a respite in the evening while you go through a chapter or two of the book. Sometimes the children will love to look at the pictures and listen to the tape. Perhaps sometimes you will want to read the captions to them. Maybe they will learn to do so and in the process learn to read. If they can already read, some of them may enjoy reading the captions aloud.

Teachers in Kindergarten and pre-school will also find the tape helpful. Perhaps you, teacher, will feel more at ease reading the material to them while the prinzes follow the book. Sometimes the children might take the parts of the animals and verbalize some of the captions.

The book is leveled at children in the pre-school and first grade level. I think that perhaps, because of the nature of the material, the child in all of us will enjoy 'TA for Tots.'

HEH HEH

2

You and I are people.

5

Did you Know that people are animals?

Irving—
If all those people are animals then we animals are people. right.

scratch scratch

Glarp!

...and that baby...

...hippopotomusses......baby turtles

and even baby chipmunks.......

...and even baby chipmunks.......

7

.....are very much... ...like baby people...

8

A puppy that is playing and having fun is like a little girl or boy who is playing and having fun.

9

As you read this book you will see

mice

little people

hippopotomusses

WAAAA!

and tiny turtles

10

But, what we will be talking about is

YOU

A boy or girl....a prinz

11

You and I have three people inside of us.

bossy me

acts like mom or dad

Thinking me

learns and makes sense

Feeling me

is Happy, sad, hurt, or angry, likes to play

These three make us act like we are three different people. Can you recognize the three people inside of you?

13

When I was a little boy
sometimes I would come home
all dirty. Then
I'd have a bath
and feel nice
and warm
and clean.

Mother would say...
"He's a different boy,"
and I felt different.

15

there  were times
when I was sad
grumpy, and angry,

Then Sometimes
I made sense and
I learned things,...

and there were
other times
when I was
very bossy.

For instance....This boy is teaching his puppy to sit up. Do you ever have fun like this?

Did you have fun today?

Having fun is good for you.

19

here is a little girl
playing with
her puppy.

And This boy
is laughing.

Oh!oh! looks like she got a spanking.

Hey, this little girl is crying.

21

Ah ha! now she is being bossy and spanking her doll.

Who taught her to do that?

22

which one is you? How can you
change when you want to be
one of these and not the other?

23

That's what this book is about,

finding out who you are

24

and how to be the you you want to be.

26

CHAPTER 2

PRINZES and

FROZZES

At one time all boys and girls were

PRINZES

* "Prinz" is womans Lib. for "prince" or "princess."

(REALLY MY WORD FOR BOY PRINCES AND GIRL PRINCESSES.) 29

Then along came some people
called Ma and Pa

30

who changed the little Prinzes ...

31

they wandered around feeling frozzy.

33

until later
they discovered
that WARM FUZZIES

DR. CLAUDE STEINER'S WORD FOR BEING CLOSE LIKE LOVE, KISSES, WARMTH, HOLDING, STROKING AND OTHER GOOD THINGS LIKE THAT, FROM HIS "FAIRYTALE", TRANSACTIONAL ANALYSIS BULLETIN, OCTOBER, 1970, VOL. 9, NO. 36.

34

could change them back into. ———————

PRINZES

again.

POOF!

Do you get **FROZZY** feelings?
Well, you can get your **PRINTZY**
feelings back. Get some nice
WARM PUZZLES. This book will
tell you how. So read on!

When you were born, you were a Prinz. You were able to feel, to laugh and to cry. You could eat, sleep, burp, wet....

YOU WERE IMPORTANT!

39

Everybody came when you called.

You felt good.
You were worth
a great deal. You were loved.

41

But sometimes, Mother or Father didn't come when you called or when they did come, they were angry or upset.

Then you felt bad.
This may have been
the start of your
Frozzy feelings.

Perhaps you began to feel not
good, not all right, not important,
not much worth to anyone.

"I'm no good," you may have said to yourself. You didn't know how to please your grown-ups.

maybe
you forgot.

45

When you first came here,
you were a tiny little baby, a Prinz.
People did many things to you which
felt good...

they held you,

They fed you,

They bathed you,

and played with you.

These things felt good
and because people who loved
you did them without your asking,
you began to feel...

49

You learned that big people were
nice. Later you learned to call them
by name, "Mommy" and "Daddy".
They were Prinzes, too.

You learned that if you smiled,
they would smile, too.

You could tell the difference between them. Mom was a softer Prinz than Dad. Their voices

were different. They smelled different. And they did nice things for you.

53

Dad and Mom became very important to you. When they were around, you felt good, ___

____ safe and happy.

When they were not around, you felt not good, sometimes hungry, cold, wet or afraid.

Later, you began to
want to do what they
wanted you to do.

You liked them and
felt good when
they smiled.

57

You learned to talk, to walk and to learn things they wanted you to learn.

After a while you began to act like Mom and Dad. They would smile at this and you would feel happy.

just like a Prinz.

59

61

How do we get to feel good? If people rub your back or smile and say "Hi," they are giving you strokes.

Strokes are what people do
or say to other people to
make them feel.

63

Good strokes give us
warm feelings.
Feelings of
being OK.
of being loved,

ROCK-A-BY MY BABY SWEET

We call those warm feelings

WARM FUZZZIES

But there is another kind of stroke – a bad stroke

Hurt feelings come from bad strokes

(like a spanking).

SWAP!
SWAP!

WAAA!

When I get a bad stroke,
I feel not O.K. - I get
shivers up my back.

BRRRR

COLD PRICKLIES

So there are two kinds
of strokes.
Strokes which
feel good
are called WARM FUZZIES

68

Strokes which feel bad are called

COLD PRICKLIES

When I pet my cat, he purrs.
He likes to be stroked. I feel
good because I've
given him a
WARM FUZZY
and he feels happy.

RUMBLE!
RUMBLE!

70

When I pat my dog on his head, he wags his tail to tell me, "Thank you, that feels good." Those are strokes that you can give with your hands.

Do you like to have your back SCRATCHED?

Ahhh! That feels good. That's another WARM FUZZY we can give with our hands.

But, we get "different strokes from different folks".

What we say and the way we look at each other cause feelings just as touch strokes do.

Hellos,

good-byes,

smiles and frowns

are strokes.

Try this:

Give everyone around you a

Tell about it.

How did you do it?
How did you feel?
How did they feel?

Did you feel good too?

Can you tell somebody something nice about them? Do that now.

By giving  good strokes to others you can feel good too.

You can give Warm Fuzzies by doing something nice for someone or by being the way they want you to be. Then they will give you strokes, too.

HAVE A COOKIE WUPPER.

THANK YOU ROCKO!

How can you get a Warm Fuzzy? One way is to ask for one. Say, "Mommy,... please hold me, I want a   WARM FUZZY"  or "Please rub my back."

Have you ever done something
to get a "COLD PRICKLIE"
A bad stroke ? Did you get
spanked or yelled at or hit ?

How did that happen ?

82

Talk about that.
How did you feel?
Tell what happened.

Sometimes people are afraid they won't get "good" strokes so they try to make other people give them bad strokes by behaving badly.

They try to make others feel unhappy or uncomfortable. Does that ever happen at your house? Talk about that and tell what you can do instead of getting Cold Pricklies.

Hey Gordon! You're O.K.

86

CHAPTER 4

FEELING GOOD AND FEELING BAD

87

People sometimes send two
messages when they talk to me.

The other day I was feeling very
unhappy and someone said to me,
"Don't feel bad, you have so
much to be happy about."

They meant – please look happy so I can feel better.

But I didn't feel like that.

89

Has your mother ever said to you

softly, when you pass someone on crutches, "Don't look at him!" She was sending you two messages. The first was,

"Don't look."

The second silent message was,

"If you look the man will feel bad."

Your feelings are as real as your big toe. Do you need a reason to have a big toe? It's a part of you and your feelings are a part of you, they are real.

You don't need a reason to be angry, hurt or afraid.

If you are not happy, you have a

Sniff snorf

right to feel your unhappiness and to talk about it.

93

Sometimes you get angry. Your anger is real. You have a right to feel angry and to tell other people about it.

Talking about it
helps you be
less angry and
to be happier
afterwards.

I: Gordon! I am angry about what you
   are doing.

G: Golly Irving - you are upset about
   something I'm doing. I want to
   hear about it.

I: Gordon! you have been <u>standing</u>
   on my tail for ten minutes!

Do you ever feel
like singing
or laughing
just because
you feel good ?

96

Enjoy it, it's OK to laugh!
That's a Warm Fuzzy feeling.

When you have
good feelings
tell people about
them too.
You don't need
a reason
to be happy.

98

WHOOPEEE!
WHOOPEE!

99

Sometimes things happen you don't like. You have the right to be angry without being afraid of being punished.

You have a right to tell Mommy or Daddy what you don't like about what they are doing.

Mommy! Daddy I don't like you to fight!

Sometimes they will change
if they can, so tell them how
you feel.

Sometimes they have to do
things you don't like because
they're good for you. But that
doesn't mean they don't love you.

If you are sick and must stay in

102

bed you can say, "I don't _like_ this, I don't _like_ being kept in bed."

You don't have to smile politely and pretend you like it to please others.

What you may have to do is stay in bed because you are sick.

Another time brother or sister
may do something you don't like.

You have a right to say, "I don't like that. I get unhappy when you do that."

But, you don't have the right to hit him or her. Hitting is very bad for people.

OUCH!
Hitting is harmful to kids and other living things.

When you were little
and hungry, you cried.
Mommy fed you
and you felt better.

Sometimes,
when you
were angry
or afraid,
she fed you.

Sometimes now when you feel angry or afraid or hurt, you may eat to feel better.

chonk! chonk!

This is not the best way of dealing with your feelings.

A better way is to talk about your uncomfortable feelings with someone who will listen.

Some people handle their "awful" feelings in a crooked way. They are afraid to tell them right out.

In fact they are afraid to tell them at all.

So, instead of saying, "I'm unhappy," they have been known to wet their bed. Why is that?

What do you do when you feel sad? How do you get your angry feelings out? Slam doors? Break toys? Cry? What?

How else could you do it?

113

Happy feelings, unhappy feelings, scared feelings, angry feelings, hurt feelings. Let's talk about yours right now and see if we can find a better way for you to handle them than some of the ways we've talked about in this chapter.

Here are some things to talk about.

1. Sometimes you get angry at Mother or Father. Then you hit your brother or sister.

Did you ever do that? What can you do instead of hitting?

2. Sometimes you "get back at" them later. What is a better way?

3. Tell what you do when you feel sad. Do you cry, get angry, keep quiet, sleep?

4. What can you do when you want some Warm Fuzzies?

5. Tell me in ten words or more how you're feeling right now. I hope you feel very good and have had a lot of nice Warm Fuzzies today. Talk about them too. They are nice to remember.

CHAPTER 5

HOW A FROZ TURNED INTO A PRINZ

Today I am going to tell you a story and I'm making it up as I go along, which is kind of fun.

Once upon a time there was a beautiful, beautiful Prinz. She went out walking in a lovely woods.

121

Pretty soon as she was going through a quiet place she kicked what she thought was a stone in the path. But, the stone moved, jumped and said, "Ouch! Why did you kick me ?" can you imagine her surprise when she heard a stone speak ?

123

She turned around, looked and asked, "Who said that?" And the stone (which was really a Froz) said, "I did. You kicked me and it hurt." And the Prinz said out loud, "Oh, I'm sorry," and to herself, "That's funny. A Froz can't talk." The Froz said, "Well, I'm really a handsome young man but I have

had a magic spell put on me which turned me into a Froz."

The Prinz said,"Well I don't know what I can do about that. Sounds kind of silly, being turned into a Froz." The Froz said," You can help me if you would, Prinz; if you will pick me up and kiss me, I will turn into a Prinz, too. Then we could be friends and have fun together."

Well, against her better judge-
ment and feeling very silly (for who
ever heard of kissing a Froz) she
agreed to help him. Now this is
kind of a dumb story because, you
know, I don't see what is wrong
with being a Froz. Frozzes have
more fun than anybody. They sit on
lily pads, catch flies and swim as

much as they want. At any rate this Froz wanted to be a man Prinz again. So she picked him up and kissed him, making a wry little face as she did it. Do you know what a "wry little face" is? (Did you ever make a "wry little face"? Make one now. That's it.) she screwed up her face and her mouth but fortunately

it didn't
stay that way,
because she really
was pretty.

129

Of course, she was taking a big chance, because if he could change into a person by being kissed, she might get changed into a Froz by kissing him. Well, she decided to take the chance and closing her eyes, she kissed him. Lo and behold, he jumped right out of his Froz skin and became a handsome Prinz.

131

And, he was a neat fellow. So they went off and had a picnic and lots of fun. After a while they got to know each other very well and I guess they got married. I don't really know what happened after that. The thing that I want to talk about is a feeling that some people have which is very much like the one the

132

Froz had before he became a Prinz again. You know when you were first born, you were very much a Prinz. The funny part of this is that, whether you are a boy or a girl, you always start out a Prinz.
As a baby, you are OK. Everything is fine. You can think, feel, breathe, cry and laugh.

133

There is nothing wrong when you are first born. Everybody loves you and takes good care of you. Right? They rock you and pat you. They want you! After a while, so that you don't make a mess all over the place (like when you have to go to the bathroom) Mother and Dad try to teach you how to control yourself.

When you don't learn as fast as they want you to, they begin to tell you things that lead you to feel less and less like a Prinz and more and more like a clumsy Froz.

You begin to change
your feelings, until soon
you begin to feel
you are a Froz
instead of the
Prinz you were.
That's where the
idea of a "spell"
came from. From you.
136

You say, "Gee, I'm a mess. I can't do anything right. I can't please anybody. Everybody is against me. They are all Prinzes and I'm just a messy little Froz."

tears

And *it is* pretty bad being a Froz or an ugly duckling when everyone else (or so it seems) is a *Prinz*. You get to feel pretty bad about this.

138

What are some Frozzy feelings you have? Wow, that's scary. If I'm a Froz, I won't get any strokes. I know! I'll make believe I'm a Prinz. I'll fool people. I'll play "Look Ma, I'm the greatest." (I know I'm not.)

Hmpf!

or I'll play "I'm better than she is." That will get me strokes even though I'm a Froz. Strokes I get like that are really cold pricklies but what can I do? I'm a Froz- Boo Hoo!

Well, I want to talk to you a little bit about how you can get rid of the awful feeling of being a Froz. For you are a Prinz. The same one you were when you were born. And no matter what mistakes you have made nor how you may do things, nor how well other people do them, you are OK. You have great worth. You are important and you can think.

You are a Prinz— so away with those Frozzy feelings! I think it is very important when you have Frozzy feelings that you talk about them with Mother and Daddy, Brother, Sister, Grandma or whoever you feel cares

142

about you. And they do care!
Talking will get rid of ugly frozzy
feelings.

Doing things is
even better. Run,
jump, slide, swing,
climb, throw, skate,
swim, etc.

143

Why should you go around feeling like a Froz when you don't have to? You can feel like a Prinz best if you do Prinzy things. Do something Prinzy right now.
See if you can let me know about some of the things you are not happy about. OK, tell me one right now.

144

Now tell me a happy feeling!
Now do a happy thing.

CHAPTER 6

BEING ANGRY

Do you ever get angry?
Very, very angry? I do!

Oh! I get so angry!
sometimes I get angriest at

people I like the most.
149

Sometimes when I'm angry, I think some pretty awful things.

Some of the things I don't want anyone to know. Like, "I'd like to bash her" or "kill, kill" or maybe "I hate you."

I get so mad sometimes that I could beat everybody up.

152

But, I know I
can't say or do
these things so
I try to keep
them to myself. Then I sulk.

153

Does that ever happen to you?
I wonder why. I think there is
a reason.

You're afraid that if you tell
Mommy and Daddy how angry you
are, they may stop loving you.

154

You don't want to take a chance on losing the good strokes they give you.

I know they'll love you no matter what you tell them but if you're not sure of that, you get afraid to say how you feel.

What do you do with the anger you feel towards your Mother, Daddy, brother, sister or grandma when they take something away from you and won't give it back?

157

Do you get very angry when you can't have what you want; can't go out and play; have to go to bed before you're ready?

Do you get as mad as I did when my sister called me and said, just when I was coming up to bat. "Maurice, Mommy says, 'Come in this instant,'!"

159

Then they would say,
"Don't show your temper to me.

Don't you dare talk back."

161

Here are a series of things that mothers and dads sometimes say when they want you to keep your feelings in.

They say,
"You keep a <u>stiff</u> <u>upper</u> <u>lip</u>."
(How do you do that? make a stiff upper lip. it's not easy.)

162

Then they say,
"Now you wipe
off the frown
and smile."

Try frowning and
smiling at the
same time. That's
pretty rough, too.

163

Now if you really want to do something hard, try keeping a stiff upper lip and drinking through a straw while you smile and frown— all at the same time. Wow!

stiff upper lip →

164

Another time, grown-ups will say,
"Smile. Don't frown."
Even if you feel awful they want
you to smile.

I know some grown-up people who smile even when they feel so bad they want to cry, or so angry they want to hit someone.

What can you do when you feel bad? Should you keep smiling and hide your feelings and look happy?

166

167

Some people I know do this. In order to keep their anger in they hurt themselves. They bite their nails. They scratch themselves.

CHOMP
CHOMP
CHOMP

SCRATCH

SCRATCH
SCRATCH

167½

They pull their hair.

Mommy, I don't feel good.

They even get sick at their stomach.

Some eat too much and get fat.

168

These things don't work,
and they hurt.

All you have to do to feel better
is talk about how you feel.
You'll feel better right away.

169

Remember,
feelings are just as real
as noses and toeses.

So, let your feelings come out.
You'll feel better, be happier
and so will everybody else.

170

There are only two things to remember:

1. find someone who cares to listen to your feelings.

2. don't dump your feelings on little people.

Another way to get rid of your angry feeling is to hit pillows. You can have neat temper tantrums in your room and not hurt anyone. You could pound clay, hammer your peg board, throw bean bags ...

OSCAR

ZAPPO!

Or if you can find a safe place, throw clods of mud that won't hurt anybody. You can throw them at a tree, makes a nice thud.

What are some other ways that we can get out anger without hurting anybody or ourselves?

Talk about that.

174

There is nothing wrong with saying

"I'm angry!"

177

CHAPTER 7

BEING AFRAID
AND
WHAT TO DO ABOUT IT

178

Lots of boys and girls are frightened
by a lot of things.
Did you know that?
Lots of grown-ups, too. I often feel
frightened. Lots of people do.

People are frightened about

181

being left alone

or being alone in the dark

183

185

don't know

or being jumped out at.
187

188

These are scary feelings. I guess you can see that the things we are afraid of most **are** being alone and not being safe.

One way to get over feeling afraid is to go to **people** you feel care about you and who give you good strokes.

Tell them your fears and then you
will not feel alone anymore.
190

But, you say, "I can't tell anybody I'm afraid. They'll laugh at me."

Not if they care and are wise. So be sure and pick someone who likes you and is wise.

191

One of the biggest fears that we have is talking about our feelings.

"I want to talk."

"I'm afraid to talk."

these two ideas fight each other.

192

If I'm afraid to talk about my feelings, I have to keep 'em to myself. If I keep 'em to myself, I'm all alone with 'em.

So you must select somebody who won't make fun of you, who will listen and keep on loving you even though you are afraid.

193

One thing for sure, nobody else can know about your feelings if you don't tell them. If you don't tell, you are left alone with the scary things.

194

So, tell people who care about you how you feel. Find someone who cares about you, Mommy, Daddy, a friend, Grandmom or Grandpa.

People like me (who wrote this book) practice listening and understanding people's feelings.

So, if you are too afraid to talk to Mommy and Daddy about your feelings, maybe you can come in and talk to me or somebody like me.

196

That's a good thing to do, too,
because you'll have another friend
and feel lots better.
197

A friend is
somebody who likes you
and whom you like.

Fear of being alone, alone with your feelings of anger, fear or hurt, is most uncomfortable.

Talk to people who care and you'll feel better.

A good friend of mine, Eric Berne, M.D., once said,

199

"Old friends are good to have. So the sooner you start making new friends the sooner you will have old friends."

One way to have a friend is to trust him with a secret.

200

201

CHAPTER 8

MIXED
AND
UNMIXED

Once upon a time I knew someone who got all mixed-up.
   He got that way because his Daddy and Mommy, while they loved him very much, often told him to do two different things at the same time.

   For instance, look what happened one evening:

203

It was like they were saying "yes" and "no" at the same time.

Does that ever happen at your house?

If so what can you do? What can Mommy and Daddy do?

Another time, at a restaurant, Wupper wasn't hungry and wouldn't eat his food. Mom and Dad were angry with him. Mother said, in an angry voice, "Eat your food! Don't be so stubborn!"

206

What does that word "stubborn" mean? Wupper did not know. But mom was so angry, he thought it must be something bad.

But then, much to his surprise, Mom laughed and said to Dad, "Oh! Wupper is so <u>stubborn!</u> He's just like you!" Daddy laughed too.

Now Wupper was mixed-up again. First they were angry and said, "Don't be stubborn" and then they talked as if they liked him to be stubborn. What does "stubborn" mean anyway?

208

I know a mixed-up
little girl who told lies.

Her mother told her
mixed-up things like:

210

The little girl decided that she could still do things she had been told not to do as long as she didn't let her mother catch her.

This seemed like
a pretty neat idea,
but it wasn't.

211

The little girl was
unhappy and always
afraid something awful
would happen if
mother found out.

212

Another mother and father often told their children it was wrong to tell lies.

Never tell lies, Mabel.

But then, sometimes the parents would do strange things: like the day a lady came to the door and asked,

"Is your Mother home?"

Mother didn't want to talk to the lady.

"Just say your Mommy is not home" she told one of the children. This mixed the child up. If it was wrong to tell lies, then why did mom want her to lie to the lady at the door?

Mom, A Lady wants to see you.

Oh! A saleswoman! Tell her I'm not home.

215

How can we keep from getting mixed-up? Well, one thing is to know that mommies and daddies get mixed-up, too.

Like everyone else, they have feelings—

and sometimes they say and do things without thinking.

216

... just like you say angry things that you don't mean later when you're not angry.

Here's a mixed-up message:

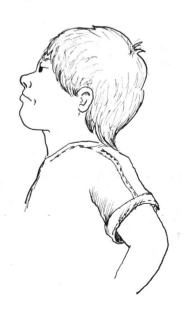

Just don't get too smart, buster.

"Don't get too smart."

Dad doesn't mean, "Don't be bright,"

what he means is:

"I don't like it when
you talk back to me."

218

Here's another one:

What she means is:
"I don't like you to do that. I'm afraid you'll fall down and get hurt."

219

so, sometimes
daddies and mommies
"say" things
that they don't mean.

Another thing that mixes boys and girls up is when mommies and daddies fight.

Most Moms and Dads love each other, we know that. But, they have fights and act as if they hate each other.

221

What we don't know is that
mothers and fathers can disagree
and be angry with each other
and still love each other.

222

Remember –
it's all right to have angry, hurt
or afraid feelings.

When you feel mixed-up,
remind yourself:

"I'm O.K." and "They're O.K.".

(O.K. means that you are able to think. You have great worth and you're important to other people and to yourself.)

To get un-mixed, talk about the things you are mixed-up about.

225

Once upon a Froz, a long Witch ago, in the land of Okay, lovely Prinzes rode down the forest trails laughing and singing.

They were happy
because in okay,
everyone was (O.K.).
228

They were O.K. because they knew they were worth a great deal and all the other Okayans were important, kind and loving.

Okayans were healthy. In Okay, Fuzzies were free and Cold Pricklies were against the law.

The Okay Society of the World is now open for members.

Will you join?

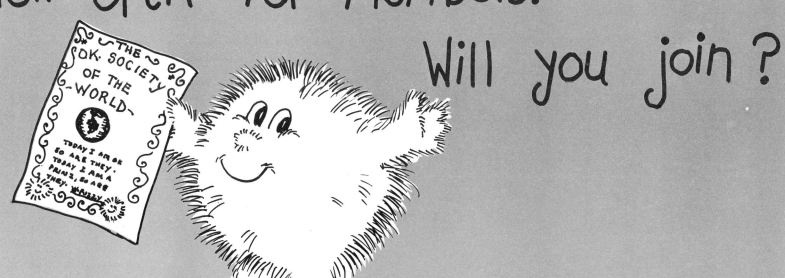

To be an Okayan, look in the magic mirror in your bathroom each morning and again before you go to bed.

Then, repeat the following magic words:

THE Warm Fuzzy CLUB

All those in favor of feeling OK and feeling loved are WARM FUZZY people. The WARM FUZZY CLUB is dedicated to keeping WARM FUZZIES alive and bouncing. You can get more WARM FUZZIES and be a WARM FUZZY person to friends and grown-ups by being a WARM FUZZY CLUB MEMBER.

When you sign up for the WARM FUZZY CLUB you get your WARM FUZZY CLUB Membership Certificate and a WARM FUZZY to wear proudly.

Then, every eight weeks there's the WARM FUZZY CLUB NEWS. The NEWS is written by Dr. and Mrs. Alvyn M. Freed, psychologist, lecturer and author of TA for TOTS, TA for KIDS, and TA for TEENS. Dr. Freed will tell you how to be happier and how to make other people happier with winning WARM FUZZY ways. You'll find out about special WARM FUZZY games and contests, too. Your parents and friends will want to share the WARM FUZZY NEWS because it always contains sprightly, helpful suggestions from Dr. Freed and Marge Freed.

WARM FUZZY CLUB members will receive a free WARM FUZZY, I'm OK full color poster (18" x 24")*. This colorful poster has the wonderful Today, I'm OK poem reprinted from TA for TOTS. The beautiful poster is ringed by all the funny, lovable characters from Dr. Freed's books.

As WARM FUZZY CLUB members you'll be the first to know about new books in the WARM FUZZY series by JALMAR PRESS and you'll be able, if you wish, to take advantage of special offerings before the books or WARM FUZZY mementoes are distributed to the public.

There will be other offerings to club members such as WARM FUZZY ID buttons, WARM FUZZY T-Shirts and more exciting posters. So, if you want to keep WARM FUZZIES alive and bouncing, and forever banish COLD PRICKLIES from OK Land the WARM FUZZY CLUB IS FOR YOU.

❋ **SIGN HERE FOR YOUR WARM FUZZY CLUB MEMBERSHIP**

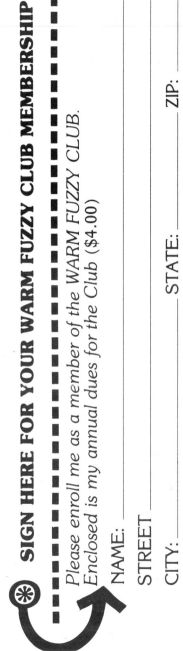

Please enroll me as a member of the WARM FUZZY CLUB. Enclosed is my annual dues for the Club ($4.00)

NAME: _____

STREET _____

CITY: _____ STATE: _____ ZIP: _____

MAIL TO: **WARM FUZZY CLUB**
JALMAR Press, Inc.,
6501 Elvas Ave.,
Sacramento, Ca. 95819

All About Your Feelings
a new LP Record Album — $5.95

Entertaining fun songs inspired by the best-selling book, TA for TOTS. Helps kids get along with kids. Brings parents and kids closer. Sample songs: Hitting is Harmful — Being Scared — When I'm Angry — Warm Fuzzy Song — Why Don't Parents Say What They Mean — I'm Not Perfect (Nobody's Perfect).

Full Color Poster features the delightful cartoon characters from TA for Tots. 18" x 24".

— $1.00

Rollicking eyes and paddle feet. Ideal for home, classroom or meeting.

50¢ each

Minimum order 50 at 50¢ each.
(Less than 50 — 60¢ each.)

by Claude Steiner — $3.95

Claude Steiner (Scripts People Live) originated the concept of Warm Fuzzies and Cold Pricklies. Here, for the first time, is the original Warm Fuzzy Tale told with beautiful illustrations by JoAnn Dick.

$1.95

24 pages with delightful cartoon characters from TA for TOTS. Fun to color. Fun captions with messages for pre-school to 4th grade youngsters.

A SPECIAL PAC THAT TELLS FAMILIES THEY'RE OK AND HELPS THEM STAY THAT WAY.

— $19.95

PARENT-PAC is based on TA for TOTS (and other Prinzes) by Alvyn M. Freed, Ph.D. You'll find it fun and exciting to use at home.

PARENT-PAC INCLUDES: Parent's Manual — TA for TOTS book — 2 LP Records (or cassette) — Warm Fuzzy I'm OK 4 color poster — Warm Fuzzies.

JALMAR PRESS INC.
6501 ELVAS AVENUE
SACRAMENTO, CA 95819
(916) 451-2897

CHECK, MONEY ORDER, CREDIT CARD,
OR PURCHASE ORDER
MUST ACCOMPANY YOUR ORDER

☐ Master Charge ☐ BankAmericard/Visa

Account Number _____

Expiration Date _____

Signature _____

SPECIAL INSTRUCTIONS

All materials F.O.B. Sacramento. Include payment of shipping and handling charges with all orders. **Calif. residents must add 6% sales tax.** Prices subject to change without notice.

BILL TO: _____

STREET _____

CITY _____ STATE _____ ZIP _____

Minimum order $5.00	
Shipping, handling and insurance charges:	
under $15.00	$1.75
$15.00 to $20.00	2.25
over $20.00	2.75
TOT-PAC or KID-PAC	4.00

PO # _____

SHIP TO: _____

STREET _____

CITY _____ STATE _____ ZIP _____

ORDER FORM

ORDER	NEW BOOKS	RETAIL
	Pajamas Don't Matter — JAN. PB 0-915190-21-4	$5.95
	The Warm Fuzzy Song Book — JAN. PB 0-915190-14-1	3.95
	T.A. for Tots Coloring Book Spirit Masters PB 0-915190-18-4	3.95
	The Human Almanac — APR. PB 0-915190-23-0	9.95
	When Apples Ain't Enough — APR. PB 0-915190-24-9	4.95
	First Time Out — APR PB 0-915190-26-5	5.95
	T.A. for TOTS VOL II — MAY PB 0-915190-25-7	7.95
	BACKLIST BOOKS	
	Finding Hidden Treasure PB 0-915190-16-8	6.95
	Hope for the Frogs PB 0-915190-17-6	3.95
	Joy of Backpacking PB 0-915190-06-0	5.95
	The Parent Book PB 0-915190-15-X	9.95
	Reach for the Sky PB 0-915190-13-3	7.95
	T.A. for Kids (3rc edition) PB 0-915190-09-5	4.95
	T.A. For Kids (in Spanish) PB 0-915190-09-5	7.50
	T.A. for Management PB 0-915190-05-2	6.95
	T.A. for Teens PB 0-915190-03-6	7.95
	T.A. for Tots PB 0-915190-12-5	7.95
	T.A. for Tots HC 0-915190-11-7	11.95
	T.A. for Tots (in Spanish) PB 0-915190-12-5	8.95
	T.A. for Tots Coloring Book PB 0-8431-0229-2	1.95
	A Time to Teach, A Time to Dance HC 0-915190-04-4	8.95
	The Original Warm Fuzzy Tale PB 0-915190-08-7	3.95

ORDER	SPECIAL TA MATERIALS	RETAIL
	Becoming the Way We Are — Levin	2.95
	Introduce Yourself to TA — Campos & McCormick	1.25
	Introduce Your Marriage to TA — Campos & McCormick	1.50
	TA Made Simple — Steiner	1.00
	The OK Game	9.95
	Warm Fuzzy Club Membership	4.00
	A/V MULTIMEDIA PAC'S	
	SOMETHING ELSE	165.00
	KID-PAC	165.00
	TOT-PAC ☐ filmstrips ☐ slides (add $15.00 for slides)	135.00
	Parent-PAC ☐ record ☐ cassette	19.95
	Warm Fuzzy T-Shirts Children's Sizes— S.M.L.XL	4.95
	Adult Sizes—S.M.L.XL	5.95
	CASSETTES, RECORDS, POSTERS	
	TA for Tots 55 minute ☐ Cassette or ☐ LP 2 Record Album	9.95
	TA for Kids 45 minute Cassette	9.95
	TA for Teens 45 minute Cassette	9.95
	TA for Management 45 minute Cassette	9.95
	Songs of the Warm Fuzzy LP Album (all about your feelings)	5.95
	Relax for Health Cassettes	
	Side A — Introduction to Hypnosis Side B — Induction. Weight Control	9.95
	Side A — Introduction to Hypnosis Side B — Induction. Tobacco Control	9.95
	Side A — Introduction to Hypnosis Side B — Induction. Ego Strengthening	9.95
	Today I'm OK 4 color Poster	1.00
	Warm Fuzzies (min. order 50)	6/5.00
	TA Growth and Development Chart	50 ea.
	Minimum order $5.00 Subtotal	.95
	CA Residents Add Sales Tax	
	Add Shipping/Handling	
	Total	